Cool Salsa

Cool Salsa

Bilingual Poems on Growing Up Latino in the United States

edited by **Lori M. Carlson**

introduction by **Oscar Hijuelos**

Henry Holt and Company
New York

Acknowledgments

During the preparation of this book, certain individuals assisted me in special ways. I thank translators Alexandra López, Lyda Aponte de Zacklin, Johanna Vega, María Rosa Fort, and Eugenio Cano, and poetry enthusiasts Michael Evans-Smith, Luis J. Rodríguez, and Carlos Cumpián. My heartfelt appreciation to my parents and sister; my friends Beatriz López Pritchard and Frank MacShane; my agent, Renée Cho; and my editor *extraordinario* Marc Aronson, as well as his assistant, Andrew Packer. Last but certainly not least, my constant gratitude to Oscar Hijuelos.

Henry Holt and Company, Inc., *Publishers since 1866*
115 West 18th Street, New York, New York 10011
Henry Holt is a registered trademark of Henry Holt and Company, Inc.

Published in Canada by Fitzhenry & Whiteside Ltd.,
195 Allstate Parkway, Markham, Ontario L3R 4T8.
Library of Congress Cataloging-in-Publication Data
Cool salsa: bilingual poems on growing up Latino in the United States /
edited by Lori M. Carlson; introduction by Oscar Hijuelos.
    p.   cm.—(An Edge book)
    1. Children's poetry, American—Hispanic American authors—Translations into Spanish.   2. Children's poetry, Hispanic American (Spanish)—Translations into English.   3. Children's poetry, American—Hispanic American authors.   4. Children's poetry, Hispanic American (Spanish)   5. Hispanic American children—Juvenile poetry.   6. American poetry—Hispanic American authors.   7. Hispanic American youth—Juvenile poetry.   8. Hispanic Americans—Juvenile poetry.   I. Carlson, Lori M. II. Series: Edge books.   PS591.H58C66   1994   811'.540809282—dc20   93-45798
ISBN 0-8050-3135-9 / First Edition—1994
Printed in the United States of America on acid-free paper.∞
10 9 8 7 6

acknowledged:
)ermission from the publisher
Press, University of Houston,
rinted by her permission.
' Copyright © by E. J. Vega.

.buelito Who." Reprinted by
d Ways by Sandra Cisneros.

    Johanna Vega for her poem "A Puerto Rican Girl's Sentimental Education." Copyright © by Johanna Vega. Reprinted by her permission.
    Luis Alberto Ambroggio for his poem "Comunión," retitled "Learning English." Copyright © by Luis Alberto Ambroggio. Reprinted by his permission.
    Sandra M. Castillo for her poem "Pork Roast." Copyright © by Sandra M. Castillo. Reprinted by her permission.
    Cristina Moreno for her poem "Take Me Down to the Mexican Moon." Copyright © by Cristina Moreno. Reprinted by her permission.

In memory of my grandparents,
Blaine and Alida Carlson,
and Francesca Forte

Contents

Editor's Note

BY LORI M. CARLSON

I grew up in a small town where the redbrick streets had names like Myrtle and Forest. The surnames of my friends were Swedish, English, and Italian. My town was encircled by woodland, far from the city, but the local board of education was sophisticated; it understood that foreign-language study was important, a privilege. And so, at the age of nine, I began to take Spanish lessons at Fletcher Elementary School. There were five or six of us eager kids who met twice a week in a cheerful oak-paneled library and learned the basics of this roller-coaster, fast-beat language that would open up a world of wonder, travel, friendships—an expansion of my life in every way.

In junior high and high school my love of the Spanish language and the cultures to which it was linked grew fast. Few Latin Americans or Latinos lived in Jamestown, New York, in the 1970s. But one Puerto Rican girl in my Spanish class, Elba Ruíz, became my friend, and she and I began a Spanish club for students who wanted to become more familiar with the culture and literature.

In high school we read Spain's poets but rarely, if ever, Latin American poets. (I wonder how Elba felt about that.) Poets such as Gustavo Aldofo Bécquer and Góngora were the curriculum's writers of choice, not the poets of South

America, Mexico, or the Caribbean Basin. Spanish, in those days, meant Spain.

Now, nearly twenty years later, years spent studying and writing about Latin American literature and making it my profession, I marvel at how vibrant and alive the Latino presence is in the United States. Although the Spanish language and Ibero-Latin American heritage have been a part of this nation's history from the very beginning, we are finally celebrating these influences. This anthology, I hope, will contribute to an even greater appreciation and understanding of Latinos in cities such as Chicago, New York, Detroit, Los Angeles, Houston, Denver, and Miami. The poets in this book are representative of the whole of the United States, not just the east and west coasts.

I hope *Cool Salsa* also helps to encourage language study. Speaking more than one language, I have found, enriches life, broadens perspective, extends horizons of opportunity, and makes us more sensitive to nuance, difference, contrast. In this anthology, the reader will encounter the beat and pulse, the *sabor* of first-generation, second-generation, and even third-generation U.S. writers of Latin American heritage. The poems are just as diverse. They are about struggling to survive and finding respect, about dating and family, dreams and future plans, hot dogs, and orange trees. There is no predominant style in these poems either. Some of the verse is traditional and lyrical, while other work is written in free verse or the voice of the streets. I searched throughout the country for the best Latino writing in any language; to my surprise, most of the poetry on young-adult themes was originally written in English, not Spanish. If you try reading each poem in both languages, one after the other, you will see very different pictures. Yet even when Latino writers use English, Spanish is often there in their rhythms, words, and ideas. The poems here are presented bilingually, with the exception of a few whose very essence is derived from being written in both languages, not necessarily Spanglish but definitely an English-Spanish mix.

Poetry translation—all literary translation—serves to share the artistry and meaning of one language and one culture with another; a kind of binoculars through which we see two different *vistas*. For this reason the Spanish is sometimes as fractured as the English and peppered with individual and regional slang as well as syntax. The Spanish in this book reflects the wide cultural diversity of the people who speak it. Rather than try to translate poems such as "Bato Loco!" or "Día de los muertos," these poems appear in their original form, without translation. They should be appreciated as much for their mixed language as their clear message. Can it not be that some ideas, some expressions, some emotions, are more aptly conveyed in one language than another? *Cool Sauce* or *Cool Sass* just is not *Cool Salsa*!

Introduction

BY OSCAR HIJUELOS

I was born in 1951, in New York City, to Cuban parents. My mother and father had immigrated in a spirit of adventure, to find—as is often documented, beaten into the ground—"a new life." They had arrived from Oriente province Cuba in the 1940s with, as the copy on the back of my first novel, *Our House in the Last World*, said about our fictional counterparts, a "suitcase packed with dreams." Both had graduated from their high schools in their respective towns in Cuba—Holguín and Jiguaní—and both were young and much uninformed about their true prospects in this country. My father, Pascual, was a hotel cook and eventually worked himself to death, and my mother, Magdalena, was a housewife. When I was a kid my mother seemed to epitomize the confusion and unsettling loneliness of the immigrant who does not know much of the English language or have a profession. I have specific memories: sitting with my mother and reading comics—what she called "funny books"—together, I suppose the two of us learning to read English at the same time, my mother struggling with certain words. And here is another: my mother taking me to a clinic and feeling panicked because the nurses did not speak Spanish, a voice repeating, "Now you sit down! You know what 'sit down' means. I said *sit down* and you will be called." Or the fact that in the hallway of our building on 118th Street, our mailbox had the name of Basulto instead of Hijuelos on the buzzer, because my parents' names were not on the lease. For years and years we knew that the name should be changed, but somehow couldn't be changed, because the landlord might then pass some judgment on our suitability as tenants and evict us. Multiply these simple but dislocating experiences by a thousand and know that they are far away and nowhere as vivid in my mind now as they were then, and you can have a vague idea of what it's like to be raised with a feeling of what I will call "second classness."

Of course, now, years later, at eighty, my mother claims New York as her one and only home, recalling Cuba mainly through childhood memories and her memories of friends. And at the same time she is perfectly delighted with the fact that she has long become acquainted with her new life. It seems simple, but just knowing where things are and how things get done are immense comforts to her; she has a hospital, a drugstore, church, and post office to go to, and she has her friends (Latinas and Americans—"I know everybody," she boasts), citizenship, voting rights (she is a diehard Democrat), and an apartment lease in the name "Hijuelos," which my older brother and I finally arranged some ten years ago.

And yet, when I'm around her, I can notice that she still retains the habit of fear that comes with being an immigrant; a fear that she will be evicted if she does not pay her rent on time, that they will turn off the lights if she does not pay the electric bill, that the government, as overwhelming to her now as it was when she first arrived in 1943, will persecute and evict her from this world. That panic, which characterized my parents' lives, was what I was raised with; an unrelenting, unending sense of second classness that is perhaps common to all immigrants, but that was certainly enhanced by the gut feeling that we were not, nor ever would be, the inheritors of this earth, this America.

As a teenager and a young man those feelings left me baffled. Because those conditions made for suffering, and I could simply not understand why my mother and father, who were good human beings, were always so troubled, or why, as I got older, I wanted to run in the opposite direction from them. That is common enough among young people, but in my instance, my desire to escape was complicated by the longtime feeling that I had already been cut off from my family.

I was born of two Cubans. Both were dark haired, and both fair skinned, or *muy blanquito*, dark browed, while my brother and I were the recipients (as I have an entire side of the family who is like us) of some Irish blood, namely on my father's side: his maternal grandmother, a Cuban who married an Irishman, was named Concepción O'Connor; so in the world of New York in the 1950s, when the popular image of Latinos was hooked up with Xavier Cugat and Desi Arnaz, my brother (his nickname was "Pinky") and I were born with freckles, reddish blond hair, and milky skin. Not that I can remember ever having a clue to there being a difference between us and other Latinos—we did not think in that way—only that (in my memory) my father would come home with some friends from his job at the Biltmore, and that after a few eye-squinting drinks, a pal would tap my father's shoulder and ask, checking me out, "And this is really your son?" I feel a deep affection for that distant period, one that, however, was followed by a time of darkness. What happened? During a visit to Cuba I contracted a serious kidney disease and, upon returning to the States, spent nearly two years in hospitals. As my mother put it, "You went into the hospital speaking Spanish, and came out speaking English." When I came out and learned to read English with my mother, I was much in a state of shock, and while my parents seemed intent on making sure that I was okay, they did not seem bent on changing my English ways and, while addressing me in Spanish, accepted my responses in English.

There I was, speaking English in a working-class immigrant household where there were not very many books, nor for that matter, much of a direction to go into. My friends called me "El Cubano," even though I didn't look it, and there was always that growing reticence—maybe a resentment—on my part about that language, Spanish, which surrounded me, was no longer a direct part of me, and which seemed to so hold back my parents and was a source of their fears. So I entered the world, experienced a more or less typical troubled-wonderful-dangerous New York childhood. Moving like a spy through the world, I would overhear tough Bronx Irish kids talking about the "spics" on the Fordham Road bus, feel pissed at them, and, a few hours later, I'd find myself getting chased along the streets of Manhattan by the Latinos who had decided to shake down "Whitey" (me). Then I turned around one day, at the age of eighteen, to find that my father had dropped dead from overwork (two jobs, twenty-five years) and that my mother was flung into an ever deeper state of panic. I was young enough to believe that certain feelings of anger, shame, and inadequacy were escapable, and so I left home, never really returning—though I always saw my mother— until I stumbled upon a way of understanding that life through the written word.

Even the term or phrase "written word" sounds pretentious to me, as I write it now. That's not even close to the truth: I spent years blindly stumbling around, dropping in and out of school, playing music, hanging out—more or less a mad man, with these "noises" from the past in my head. I went to college because I remembered my father telling me, "If you don't want to be an elevator operator, go to school." But I found little to interest me until one day, in a prose-writing class, I made a few sentences that, in their way, seemed accomplished and interesting—in fact, that is the first time in my life that I can remember feeling that I had done anything well. While I would manage an interesting turn of phrase, and rather primitive ones at that, though, I didn't have any kind of vision or voice in my head, just a lot of static, filled with Spanish, with fears, with that panic. (I even now think of that strange term "Hispanic" as meaning His-Panic.) Yet I had much good luck on my side, a head filled with questions, and an interest in proving that I could do something well. I supposed that my half-assedness in Spanish led to an ambition in English, that walking between two worlds, I shifted to one side, though angrily so, as there was much that I did not understand about my life and began writing to discover my feelings about it.

I published my first novel, *Our House in the Last World*, in late 1983; the second, *The Mambo Kings Play Songs of Love*, in 1989; and the third, *The Fourteen Sisters of Emilio Montez O'Brien*, in 1993. The first of these books, *Our House*, I think, pretty much elaborates, in a more interesting way, upon the feelings of identity and second classness that I experienced in my early years.

Cool Salsa touches upon similar issues. It also opens doors to possibilities of thought and feeling in a way no book could do for me when I was growing up, because there were no books that addressed our world back then. Hearing one language on the streets, another at home, and a third at school, I had to find my own words, my own rhythms, my own story. So have these poets; each uses his or her own blend of Spanish, English, and everything in between. But they have the good fortune of appearing twice, speaking simultaneously in two tongues; speaking to us with their hearts and their minds at the same time.

Cool Salsa

School Days

English con Salsa

BY GINA VALDÉS

Welcome to ESL 100, English Surely Latinized,
inglés con chile y cilantro, English as American
as Benito Juárez. Welcome, muchachos from Xochicalco,
learn the language of dólares and dolores, of kings
and queens, of Donald Duck and Batman. Holy Toluca!
In four months you'll be speaking like George Washington,
in four weeks you can ask, More coffee? In two months
you can say, May I take your order? In one year you
can ask for a raise, cool as the Tuxpan River.

Welcome, muchachas from Teocaltiche, in this class
we speak English refrito, English con sal y limón,
English thick as mango juice, English poured from
a clay jug, English tuned like a requinto from Uruapán,
English lighted by Oaxacan dawns, English spiked
with mezcal from Juchitán, English with a red cactus
flower blooming in its heart.

Welcome, welcome, amigos del sur, bring your Zapotec
tongues, your Nahuatl tones, your patience of pyramids,
your red suns and golden moons, your guardian angels,
your duendes, your patron saints, Santa Tristeza,
Santa Alegría, Santo Todolopuede. We will sprinkle
holy water on pronouns, make the sign of the cross
on past participles, jump like fish from Lake Pátzcuaro

on gerunds, pour tequila from Jalisco on future perfects,
say shoes and shit, grab a cool verb and a pollo loco
and dance on the walls like chapulines.

When a teacher from La Jolla or a cowboy from Santee
asks you, Do you speak English? You'll answer, Sí,
yes, simón, of course. I love English!

And you'll hum
a Mixtec chant that touches la tierra and the heavens.

Translating Grandfather's House

BY E. J. VEGA

According to my sketch,
Rows of lemon & mango
Trees frame the courtyard
Of Grandfather's stone
And clapboard home;
The shadow of a palomino
Gallops on the lip
Of the horizon.

The teacher says
The house is from
Some Zorro
Movie I've seen.

"Ask my mom," I protest.
"She was born there—
Right there on the second floor!"

Crossing her arms she moves on.

Memories once certain as rivets
Become confused as awakenings
In strange places and I question
The house, the horse, the wrens
Perched on the slate roof—
The roof Oscar Jartín
Tumbled from one hot Tuesday,
Installing a new weather vane;
(He broke a shin and two fingers).

Classmates finish drawings of New York City
Housing projects on Navy Street.
I draw one too, with wildgrass
Rising from sidewalk cracks like widows.
In big round letters I title it:

GRANDFATHER'S HOUSE

Beaming, the teacher scrawls
An A+ in the corner and tapes
It to the green blackboard.

To the green blackboard.

Traduciendo la casa de mi abuelo
Translated from the English by Johanna Vega

En mi dibujo,
Árboles de limón y mango
Enmarcan el patio
De la casa de madera y piedra
De mi abuelo;
La sombra de un palomino
Galopa sobre el labio
Del horizonte.

La maestra dice que
La casa es de
Alguna película del
Zorro que he visto.

"Pregúntele a mi mamá," protesto.
"Ella nació ahí—
¡Ahí mismo en el segundo piso!"

Con los brazos cruzados, ella sigue.

Recuerdos que fueron una vez tan seguros como remaches
Se confunden con despertares
En sitios extraños y cuestiono
La casa, el caballo, los reyezuelos
Posados encima del techo de pizarra—
El techo del cual Oscar Jartín
Se cayó un martes caluroso
mientras trataba de instalar una veleta nueva;
(Se quebró la espinilla y dos dedos).

Mis compañeros de clase terminan sus dibujos de Nueva
   York,
Viviendas populares en la calle Navy.
Yo también dibujo uno, con hierbas silvestres
Que crecen en las veredas rotas como viudas.
Con letras grandes y redondas lo titulo:

LA CASA DE MI ABUELO

Radiante, la maestra garabatea
Una A+ en el margen y lo pega
en la pizarra verde.

En la pizarra verde.

Good Hot Dogs

for Kiki

BY SANDRA CISNEROS

Fifty cents apiece
To eat our lunch
We'd run
Straight from school
Instead of home
Two blocks
Then the store
That smelled like steam
You ordered
Because you had the money
Two hot dogs and two pops for here
Everything on the hot dogs
Except pickle lily
Dash those hot dogs
Into buns and splash on
All that good stuff
Yellow mustard and onions
And french fries piled on top all
Rolled up in a piece of wax
Paper for us to hold hot
In our hands
Quarters on the counter
Sit down
Good hot dogs
We'd eat
Fast till there was nothing left
But salt and poppy seeds even
The little burnt tips
Of french fries
We'd eat
You humming
And me swinging my legs

Buenos Hot Dogs

para Kiki

Translated from the English by the poet

Cincuenta centavos cada uno
Para comer nuestro lonche
Corríamos
Derecho desde la escuela
En vez de a casa
Dos cuadras
Después la tienda
Que olía a vapor
Tú pedías
Porque tenías el dinero
Dos hot dogs y dos refrescos para comer aquí
Los hot dogs con todo
Menos pepinos
Hecha esos hot dogs
En sus panes y salpícalos
Con todas esas cosas buenas
Mostaza amarilla y cebollas
Y papas fritas amontonadas encima
Envueltos en papel de cera
Para llevarlos calientitos
En las manos
Monedas encima del mostrador
Siéntate
Buenos hot dogs
Comíamos
Rápido hasta que no quedaba nada
Menos sal y semillas de amapola hasta
Las puntitas quemadas
De las papas fritas
Comíamos
Tú canturreando
Y yo columpiando mis piernas

A Puerto Rican Girl's Sentimental Education

BY JOHANNA VEGA

Your daughter didn't pass
the English reading test in second grade.
Left back like a donkey
or another number on
the red, white and blue
statistical roster.

Mrs. Rivera,
the section 8 projects
breed social dilemmas

or was it

Mrs. Hernández,
My records tell me your name is Fernández.

Systematic, elementary school
oppression, hippie teachers, granola breaks
in the classroom.

A low-income prodigy child
caught in the American cross fire,
between SATs and insular-community vocabulary.
Mami and Papi told me to pray in Spanish,
read the Scriptures, mi niña.

Memories choke my throat,
stuttering in English, crying
into my grammar textbook.
Mental deficits, developmental crises
and bowlegged walks to the school nurse.

Take the reading test over,
at the psychiatrist's office.
Diagnosis: psychedelic, psycholinguistic
genius survives the warring factions
of cultural schizophrenia.

Like Charlie Brown vs. Cantinflas
Like the Beatles vs. Menudo.
Like myself divided into myself
Like I'm a movie in subtitles.

Now my mind's tied up.
Hostage in a desert of hope and opportunity.
Dyslexic like Albert Einstein and
prolific like Cervantes' ego in prison.

La educación sentimental
de una niña puertorriqueña
Translated from the English by the poet

Tu hija no aprobó
el examen de lectura en inglés de segundo grado.
Repitió el grado como un burro,
como otro número
en la estadística azul, roja y blanca.

Señora Rivera,
los proyectos de la sección ocho
generan dilemas sociales.

o era

Señora Hernández,
Mis datos dicen que su nombre es Fernández.

Opresión sistemática en la escuela primaria,
maestros hippies, descanso para comer
en la clase.

Una niña prodigio de bajos ingresos
atrapada en el fuego cruzado norteamericano
entre los exámenes estandarizados y el vocabulario de la isla.
Mami y papi me dijeron que rezara en español.
Lea las escrituras, mi niña.

Los recuerdos ahogan mi garganta.
Tartamudeaba en inglés, lloraba
sobre el libro de gramática.
Déficits mentales, crisis de desarrollo
y caminatas con las piernas chuecas hasta la enfermería de la
  escuela.

Toma el examen de lectura otra vez
en el consultorio del psiquiatra.
Diagnóstico: genio psicodélico psicolingüístico
sobrevive a las confrontaciones bélicas
de la esquizofrenia cultural.

Como Charlie Brown contra Cantinflas
Como los Beatles contra Menudo.
Como si yo fuera una división.
Como si fuera una película doblada al inglés.

Hoy día mi mente está atada
Rehén en un desierto de fe y oportunidad.
Disléxica como el científico Albert Einstein y
Prolífica como el ego de Cervantes en la cárcel.

Learning English
Translated from the Spanish by Lori M. Carlson

Life
to understand me
you have to know Spanish
feel it in the blood of your soul.

If I speak another language
and use different words
for feelings that will always stay the same
I don't know
if I'll continue being
the same person.

Aprender el inglés

BY LUIS ALBERTO AMBROGGIO

Vida
para entenderme
tienes que saber español
sentirlo en la sangre de tu alma.

Si hablo otro lenguaje
y uso palabras distintas
para expresar sentimientos que nunca cambiarán
no sé
si seguiré siendo
la misma persona.

Home
and
Homeland

Where You From?

BY GINA VALDÉS

Soy de aquí
y soy de allá
from here
and from there
born in L.A.
del otro lado
y de éste
crecí en L.A.
y en Ensenada
my mouth
still tastes
of naranjas
con chile
soy del sur
y del norte
crecí zurda
y norteada
cruzando fron
teras crossing
San Andreas
tartamuda
y mareada
where you from?
soy de aquí
y soy de allá
I didn't build
this border
that halts me
the word fron
tera splits
on my tongue

Pig Roast

BY SANDRA M. CASTILLO

We meet in the yard at tía Estela's
by her mango trees, her avocados, guavas,
tropical fruit, by her gardenias, her lirios,
and her orchids, by her roosters and her white
patio furniture.

It is Ramoncito's first week in America.
And though forty, he keeps the diminutive
in his name and thanks her for pulling him,
her stepson, out of Cuba twenty years after she herself
was able to leave by weeding the lawn she can no longer
mow, by vasing the flowers she grows.

This ninety-degree Sunday,
he turns the pig, pokes it to check the crispness
of its crackling skin as Mother and I watch.
He offers us pieces of pig skin, smiles, tells us
it's the best part.

And in his pale blue Camden Maine T-shirt,
sneakers, Levi's, he is tío Ramón, tall, thin, dark.
He is the skinny twenty-year-old who must have sat
with me at that long dining table in Almendares,
where for dessert, tía Estela always gave me
a tablespoon of condensed milk. I was five;
Ramoncito was of military age.

I take what he offers, turn to watch him eat
the piece he has carved for himself. What do you think,
he asks. Mother tells him it is done; he agrees.
And they eat their pork pieces like it was Christmas
or New Year's Eve. I smile at Mother, try to give her
my piece without his noticing, but suddenly, we are caught
by tío Ramón and the video camera he aims at our faces
as he yells to get closer, get closer.

Ramoncito poses, proclaims himself chef, Mother smiles,
pulls me in. And I am caught—transparent, ashen.
I smile past the camera to that long, pink house
with its many rooms, to its tall windows and their
wrought iron. I eat a piece of dark pig skin
and wipe my mouth with the back of my hand.

Asado de puerco
Translated from the English by
Eugenio Alberto Cano Correa

Nos encontramos en el patio de tía Estela
junto a sus mangos, aguacates, guavas,
sus frutas tropicales, gardenias, lirios,
y sus orquídeas, sus gallos y los muebles
blancos del patio.

Es la primera semana de Ramoncito en América
y aunque haya cumplido 40 sigue usando un diminutivo por
    nombre
y le agradece a ella por haberlo sacado a él, su hijastro,
de Cuba, veinte años después de que ella misma
pudo salir, por cortar la grama que ella no puede ya
cortar, poniendo en jarrones las flores que ella cultiva.

Este domingo de noventa grados
él da vuelta al puerco, lo pincha para verificar que
el crujiente pellejo esté crocante mientras mamá y yo
    observamos.
Nos ofrece pedazos de pellejo, sonríe y nos dice
que es la mejor parte.

Y en su camiseta azulada de Camden Maine
zapatos tenis, Levi's, él es tío Ramón, alto, flaco, moreno.
Es el flaco de 20 años que debe haberse sentado
junto a mí en la larga mesa en Almendares,
donde tía Estela me daba siempre de postre
cucharadas de leche condensada. Yo tenía cinco años;
Ramoncito estaba ya de edad del servicio militar.

Yo tomo lo que me ofrece, giro para observarlo comer
el pedazo que tajó para sí mismo. ¿Qué piensas?,
me pregunta. Mamá le dice que está bien hecho;
él asiente.
Y comen sus trozos de puerco como si fuera Navidad
o Año Nuevo. Le sonrío a
mi madre, trato de darle
mi pedazo sin que él lo
note pero, de repente, tío Ramón nos descubre
y la cámara de video que apunta a
nuestras caras
mientras grita que nos acerquemos, acérquense.

Ramoncito posa, se proclama chef, mi madre sonríe,
me jala. Y estoy atrapada—transparente, ceniza.
Sonrío más allá de la cámara a aquella casa larga y rosada
con sus muchos cuartos, a sus ventanas altas y
sus hierros forjados. Como un pedazo de oscuro
pellejo de puerco y limpio mi boca con el dorso de mi mano.

Take Me Down
to the Mexican Moon

BY CRISTINA MORENO

para mi tía Toñia

take me down to the MEXICAN moon
where i used
to wash
my feet
in holy water
"CATHOLIC blood,"
my abuelita used
to call it;
where we, la familia, used
to eat rice on tortillas
like jam on bread
and
chase after cockroaches
like dancing geese;
where my tía Toñia used
to yell
at us
for opening
the screen door
and
letting
in all
the flies that looked
like dry moles
against our skin
every time
we had
the urge

to go inside
and
drink water
or
go to the bathroom
"¡ay que niños!"
she used
to say
to all the big people
in the house
never
realizing
the screen door had
HOLES
like the blankets
my hermanas and i used
to sleep under
like sweet princesas
beneath the violet skies
of our room;

take me deep to the MEXICAN moon
where my primos and i used
to play
with cold mud
like clay
and
use
TOPO-CHICO bottlecaps
for pesos.

Llévame a lo profundo
de la luna mexicana
Translated from the English by Alexandra López

llévame a lo profundo de la luna mexicana
donde yo solía
lavar
mis pies
con agua bendita
"sangre católica,"
como mi abuelita solía
decir;
donde nosotros, la familia, comíamos
arroz sobre tortillas
como jalea sobre pan
y
perseguir cucarachas
como gansos danzantes;
donde mi tía Toñia
nos gritaba
por abrir
la puerta de metal
y dejar
entrar todas
las moscas que parecían
lunares secos
sobre nuestra piel
cada vez
teníamos
ganas
de entrar
y
tomar agua

o de ir al baño
"¡ay qué niños!"
ella solía
decir
a toda la gente grande
de la casa
sin darse cuenta
nunca
de que la puerta de metal tenía
AGUJEROS
como las mantas con las cuales
mis hermanas y yo
nos cubríamos para dormir
como dulces princesas
bajo los cielos violetas
de nuestro cuarto.

llévame a lo profundo de la luna mejicana
donde mis primos y yo
jugábamos
con barro frío
como cerámica
y
usábamos
tapitas de TOPO-CHICO
como si fueran pesos.

Día de los muertos

BY ABELARDO B. DELGADO

Renacen los huertos,
también los muertos.
El día de los muertos
por siete minutos
                podemos platicar
  con los seres queridos fallecidos.
I remember
           tagging along
chasing my abuela
to el camposanto
                to sell paper flowers
to make the somber tombs bright.
That was back in Mexico.
I was only seven years old.
Here in the U.S.
              los muertos
are personas non gratas.
Here we do not wish
           to hold dialogue
with los muertos.
They remind us
          we too
will eventually join them.
Here there is no luto
and there are no novenas
or puños de tierra.
Here in the U.S.

                    the idea is to hide,
to ignore the dead
and to even avoid death
in our conversations.
In Mexico la muerte
                    is well known.
She's la talaca, a feminine figure.
Our Puerto Rican
                    brothers and sisters
call her "la flaca."
Talking with the dead is necessary
to remind ourselves
to enjoy our lives
and not to go about
as if we had already died
and no one said good-bye or cried.

Domingo Means Scrubbing

BY ALICIA GASPAR DE ALBA

our knees for Church.
'Amá splicing our trenzas tight
with ribbons, stretching
our eyes into slits. Grandpa
wearing his teeth.

Domingo means one of our tíos
passing out quarters
for the man with the basket
and me putting mine under
my tongue like the host.

Then menudo and Nina's
raisin tamales for dessert.
Our tías exchange Pepito
jokes in the kitchen
while we sneak a beer
into the bathroom,
believing the taste
will make our chi-chis grow.

Domingo means playing
a la familia with all our cousins,
me being the Dad 'cause I'm
the oldest and the only one
who'll kiss the Mom
under the willow tree.

After dark,
our grandmothers pisteando
tequila on the porch, scaring us
every little while: *La llorona
knows what you kids are doing!*
'Amá coming out of the house
to drag the girls inside
pa' lavar los dishes.

Domingo means scrubbing.

El domingo es día de fregar
Translated from the English by the poet

nuestras rodillas para ir a misa.
'Amá nos restira los ojos al trenzarnos
listones en el pelo, el Grandpa
estrena sus dientes.

El domingo uno de los tíos
reparte pesetas para el señor
de la canastita, y yo me guardo
la mía bajo la lengua como una hostia.

Luego hay menudo y de postre
los tamales dulces que hace Nina.
Las tías se cuentan chistes de Pepito
en la cocina, mientras nosotras sacamos
una cerveza a escondidas, al baño,
creyendo que el sabor nos hará crecer
las chi-chis.

El domingo es día de jugar
a la familia con todos los primos,
yo haciéndola de papá porque soy la mayor
y la única que se atreve a besar
a la mamá debajo del sauce llorón.

Al anochecer las abuelas pisteando tequila
en el patio, asustándonos a cada ratito:
La llorona sabe lo que andan haciendo, ¡malcriados!
'Amá sale de la casa
y a fuerzas nos mete a las chavalas
pa' lavar los platos.

El domingo es día de fregar.

The Changeling
BY JUDITH ORTÍZ COFER

As a young girl
vying for my father's attention,
I invented a game that made him look up
from his reading and shake his head
as if both baffled and amused.

In my brother's closet, I'd change
into his dungarees—the rough material
molding me into boy-shape; hide
my long hair under an army helmet
he'd been given by Father, and emerge
transformed into the legendary Ché
of grown-up talk.

Strutting around the room,
I'd tell of life in the mountains,
of carnage and rivers of blood,
and of manly feasts with rum and music
to celebrate victories *para la libertad.*
He would listen with a smile
to my tales of battles and brotherhood
until Mother called us to dinner.

She was not amused
by my transformations, sternly forbidding me
from sitting down with them as a man.
She'd order me back to the dark cubicle
that smelled of adventure, to shed
my costume, to braid my hair furiously
with blind hands, and to return invisible,
as myself,
to the real world of her kitchen.

Transformación
Translated from the English by Johanna Vega

Cuando era pequeña,
compitiendo por la atención de mi padre,
inventé un juego que lo hacía levantar la vista
de lo que leía y mover la cabeza
como si estuviera a la vez sorprendido y divertido.

En el armario de mi hermano, me ponía
sus pantalones—el áspero material hacía
que mi cuerpo pareciera el de un chico; escondía
mi pelo largo en el casco
que le había regalado papá y salía
transformada en el legendario Ché
de las conversaciones adultas.

Pavoneándome en el cuarto,
hablaba de la vida en las montañas,
de las matanzas y los ríos de sangre,
y de los banquetes masculinos con ron y música
para celebrar los triunfos para la libertad.
Con una sonrisa él escuchaba
mis cuentos de batallas y fraternidad
hasta que mamá nos llamaba a cenar.

A ella no le divertían
mis transformaciones, prohibiéndome severamente
que me sentara con ellos como hombre.
Me ordenaba que volviera al cubículo
que olía a aventuras para quitarme
el disfraz, para trenzarme el pelo furiosamente
con manos ciegas y que regresara invisible,
como yo misma,
al mundo real de su cocina.

My Memories of the Nicaraguan Revolution

BY EUGENIO ALBERTO CANO CORREA

A tear streaming from my eye,
Running through a field seeking refuge,
A road lined with bullet shells instead of pebbles,
An empty wheelbarrow stained red,
A pillar of smoke uniting sky and ground,
A slogan cried from the background,
A hug of protection from my *mamá*.

Mis recuerdos de la revolución nicaragüense
Translated from the English by Alexandra López

Una lágrima fluyendo de mi ojo,
Corriendo a campo traviesa buscando refugio,
Un camino marcado por balas servidas en vez de guijarros,
Una carretilla vacía manchada de rojo,
Un pilar de humo uniendo cielo y tierra,
Una consigna gritada desde el fondo,
Un abrazo protector de mi mamá.

Memories

There's an Orange Tree Out There
Translated from the Spanish by Darwin J. Flakoll

There's an orange tree out there, behind that old,
abandoned garden wall,
but it's not the same orange tree we planted,
and it's a beautiful orange tree
so beautiful it makes us remember
that orange tree we planted

                                    —in our earth—

before coming to this house
so distant and remote from that one
where we planted an orange tree
and even saw it—like this one—in flower.

Hay un naranjo ahí

BY ALFONSO QUIJADA URÍAS

Hay un naranjo enfrente, tras de ese viejo tapial
abandonado,
pero no es el mismo naranjo que sembramos,
y es un bello naranjo
tan bello que nos hace recordar
aquel naranjo que sembramos

                    —en nuestra tierra—

antes de venir a esta casa
tan distante y lejana de aquélla
donde sembramos un naranjo
y hasta lo vimos—como éste—florecer.

Memories of Uncle Pety

BY CLAUDIA QUIRÓZ

for Jaime Villarroel Roldán

I hid behind gauze-stiff curtains
and watched my aunts and uncles
play poker until two, three,
sometimes four in the morning.
In the smoke-filled dining room,
I counted diamond-pointed queens,
mustachioed jacks
and kings, and watched Uncle Pety's
red-and-blue towers topple over,
then restack themselves.
A Bic lighter, several
ashtrays, tumblers of iced rum.

Uncle Pety collapsed on a sidewalk
years later, lay unrecognized
in a public hospital.
Mother had just bought
a golden buddha—about my size then—
from an antique store in Georgetown.
For hours, I sat at my upright Baldwin,
playing sonatinas and preludes.
She wept quietly for days
in her sealed-off dining room.

I remember a tunnel, its coarse,
orange rug; a wall-sized black-and-white
reproduction of the moon; playing
in quiet loneliness.

And I dreamed of Uncle Pety
playing chess: every so often
he rubbed the small crater
on his chest, for good luck
it seemed. Once, holding my shoulder
he led me out, triumphant, bright-eyed,
tiny and wise under his spotted arm.

We drove through the city's outer husk,
up the windy road to its crumbling edge.
Gritty slabs of weathered stone,
and flowers, too. We spotted his:
dirt packed into the chiseled grooves.
Veiled women crept by mouthing
Hail Marys. I spread wildflowers
for him, raised my forefinger,
and rubbed my chest lightly: he
knew what I meant.

Recuerdos de tío Pety

Translated from the English by María Rosa Fort

Me escondía tras tiesas cortinas de gasa
y miraba a mis tías y tíos
jugar al poker hasta las dos, tres,
a veces cuatro de la mañana.
En el comedor lleno de humo,
contaba reinas de diamantes,
jacks bigotudos
y reyes, y veía cómo las torres
rojas y blancas de tío Pety se derrumbaban,
luego se reacomodaban.
Un encendedor Bic, varios
ceniceros, vasos de ron helado.

Tío Pety se desplomó sobre una vereda
años más tarde, yació sin ser reconocido
en un hospital público.
Mamá acababa de comprar
un buda dorado—casi de mi tamaño entonces—
en un anticuario de Georgetown.
Por horas, me senté frente a mi Baldwin vertical
tocando sonatinas y preludios.
Ella lloró durante días en silencio
en su comedor sellado.

Recuerdo un túnel, su tosca
alfombra naranja, una reproducción de la luna en blanco y
    negro
del tamaño de la pared; mientras tocaba
en quieta soledad.

Y soñé con tío Pety
que jugaba al ajedrez: de tanto en tanto
frotaba un pequeño cráter
contra su pecho, para la buena suerte
al parecer. Una vez, tomándome del hombro
me condujo a la salida, triunfante, los ojos brillantes,
diminuta y sabia bajo su brazo manchado de lunares.

Manejando atravesamos el cascarón exterior de la ciudad,
trepando el camino ventoso hasta sus bordes de escombros.
Placas arenosas de piedra gastada,
y flores, también. Divisamos la suya:
tierra apisonada en ranuras cinceladas.
Mujeres con velos se arrastraban voceando
avemarías. Yo desparramé flores silvestres
para él, levanté mi dedo índice,
y froté mi pecho suavemente: él sabía
lo que yo quería decir.

The Secret

BY PABLO MEDINA

There is a photograph
of my father, mother,
sister and me going up
the steps to the plane
all smiling, I holding
a book my great-uncle
had given me on Oriental art.

Be free to learn
Only that is good,
He said.

It was cold in New York.
New words made dough in my ear.
The subway burst under my feet.

When I made it to school
they thought I didn't
have a mind in English and if
you don't have a mind in English
you have a mind in nothing.

Secretly I read Poe on the ninth floor
of that hotel that smelled
of widows with their skirts up,
discovered darkness in closets
tubed hands in a boring bathroom

as the snow whorled down
pillowing the city
with soft
glass.

El secreto
Translated from the English
by Lyda Aponte de Zacklin

Hay una fotografía en la que estamos
mi padre, madre,
hermana y yo
subiendo a un avión,
todos sonriendo,
yo con un libro de arte oriental que
me regaló mi tío abuelo.

Sé libre para aprender
Sólo eso es bueno,
Dijo.

Hacía frío en Nueva York.
Las palabras nuevas crearon pasta en mis orejas.
El tren explotó bajo mis pies.

Cuando llegué a la escuela
pensaron que no tenía una mente para el inglés
y si no tienes una mente para el inglés
no tienes una mente para nada.

En secreto leía a Poe en el noveno piso
de aquel hotel que olía
a viudas con faldas levantadas,
descubría la oscuridad en los armarios
los lavamanos en una sala de baño sin gracia

mientras la nieve caía en espiral
apilándose en la ciudad
con suave
cristal.

Abuelito Who

BY SANDRA CISNEROS

Abuelito who throws coins like rain
and asks who loves him
who is dough and feathers
who is a watch and glass of water
whose hair is made of fur
is too sad to come downstairs today
who tells me in Spanish you are my diamond
who tells me in English you are my sky
whose little eyes are string
can't come out to play
sleeps in his little room all night and day
who used to laugh like the letter k
is sick
is a doorknob tied to a sour stick
is tired shut the door
doesn't live here anymore
is hiding underneath the bed
who talks to me inside my head
is blankets and spoons and big brown shoes
who snores up and down up and down up and down again
is the rain on the roof that falls like coins
asking who loves him
who loves him who?

Abuelito que

Translated from the English
by Lyda Aponte de Zacklin

Abuelito que tira monedas como lluvia
y pregunta quién lo quiere
que es masa y plumas
que es un reloj y un vaso de agua
que tiene pelo como pelusa
está muy triste para bajar hoy
que me dice en español tú eres mi diamante
que me dice en inglés tú eres mi cielo
que tiene ojitos de hilo
no puede salir a jugar
duerme en su cuartito día y noche
que se reía como la letra k
está enfermo
es una cerradura amarrada a un palo amargo
está cansado cierra la puerta
ya no vive aquí
está escondiéndose bajo la cama
que habla dentro de mi cabeza
es cobijas y cucharas y grandes zapatos cafés
que ronca arriba y abajo arriba y abajo arriba y abajo otra
    vez
es la lluvia en el techo que cae como monedas
preguntando quién lo quiere
¿quién lo quiere? quién

An Unexpected Conversion

BY CAROLINA HOSPITAL

Mother hid from us the blue and white beads
her nanny, Brígida,
had given her, and the plate of
pennies in honey under the Virgin's skirt.
She rarely spoke about the island,
never taught us to cook black beans.

Father played Stravinsky and Debussy on Sundays.
Once, he relented and taught us the *güagüancó*.
He swore, as she did, they would never go back.
He's thirty years in exile and about to retire.

Today, Mother and I sit in the garden.
She rests on the edge of a rusted swing,
speaking of reconstruction,
of roads and houses: "I know they'll
need an experienced engineer," she says looking at Dad.

I've never seen her look so young.
I've never felt so old.

Una conversión inesperada
Translated from the English by Alexandra López

Mamá escondía de nosotras las cuentas azules y blancas
que su nana, Brígida,
le había regalado, y el plato de
kilos en miel, debajo de la Virgen.
Rara vez hablaba de la isla,
y nunca nos enseñó a cocinar frijoles negros con arroz.

Papá tocaba Stravinsky y Debussy los domingos.
Una vez, accedió a enseñarnos el güagüancó.
Juró, como ella, que no regresarían jamás.
Lleva treinta años en el exilio y está a punto de retirarse.

Hoy, mamá y yo conversamos en el jardín.
Ella descansa al borde de un columpio mohoso,
hablando de la reconstrucción
de carreteras y casas: "Yo sé que necesitarán
un ingeniero con experiencia," dice, mirando a papá.

Jamás la he visto lucir tan joven.
Jamás me he sentido tan vieja yo.

Hard Times

The Monster

BY LUIS J. RODRÍGUEZ

It erupted into our lives:
Two guys in jeans shoved it
through the door—
heaving & grunting & biting lower lips.

A large industrial sewing machine.
We called it "the monster."

It came on a winter's day,
rented out of Mother's pay.
Once in the living room
the walls seemed to cave in around it.

Black footsteps to our door
brought heaps of cloth for Mama to sew.
Noises of war burst out of the living room.
Rafters rattled. Floors farted.
The radio going into static
each time the needle ripped into fabric.

Many nights I'd get up from bed,
wander squint-eyed down a hallway
and peer through a dust-covered blanket
to where Mama and the monster
did nightly battle.

I could see Mama through the yellow haze
of a single lightbulb.
She, slouched over the machine.
Her eyes almost closed.
Her hair in disheveled braids;

each stitch binding her life
to scraps of cloth.

El monstruo
Translated from the English by Lori M. Carlson

Irrumpió en nuestras vidas:
Dos tipos en jeans la empujaron
por la puerta—
jadeando & gruñendo & mordiéndose los labios.

Una enorme máquina de coser industrial.
La llamábamos "el monstruo."

Vino un día de invierno,
alquilado con el pago de mamá.
Una vez en el living
las paredes parecieron achicarse a su lado.

Pasos negros hacia nuestra puerta
con un montón de telas para que mamá cosiera.
Ruidos de guerra estallaron en el living.
Los techos temblaron. Los pisos pedorrearon.
Había interferencias en la radio
cada vez que la aguja atacó la tela.

Muchas noches me levantaba de la cama,
deambulaba por el pasillo con los ojos desviados
y espiaba a través de una manta polvorienta
el lugar donde mamá y el monstruo
libraban su batalla nocturna.

Podía ver a mamá tras la neblina amarilla
de una sola luz.
Ella, encorvada sobre la máquina.
Sus ojos casi cerrados.
Su pelo en trenzas deshechas;

cada puntada ligando su vida
a retazos de tela.

Bato Loco!

BY RAMÓN DEL CASTILLO

Bato Loco, con su cabeza
llena de mota,
lighting the paths into los barrios
dark with fear.
Can you hear as you sit
　　idly
in classrooms where
the silence of indoctrination
　　subtly
grabs you and makes
a believer of false notions
　　of inferiority
and passes judgment
about your ancestors' feathers.

Bato Loco! Your path
they tell you
is predetermined. Filled
with solemn images
where you stand behind bars
while your intestines,
filled with crack,
eat away
at your conscience
laying bare on the front streets
de sus propios barrios,
filled with homeboys, pop tarts,
gruesome realities,
nightmares caused by the ingestion
of filthy needles
shot into arms full of tattoos.

Bato Loco! Take off that handkerchief
from around your head,
and wipe away la sangre
of a thousand years of bloodshed
        y miseria
draped in an idolatrous symbol
at a time when sus carnales
estaban cantando sweet melodies
into las ears
of las rucas
about dreams that have yet
to come true.

Bato Loco! Escape from
the fires of el infierno
scorching your alma
frying you like a crispy critter
so you can become
la avena for the breakfast
        of the champions of una sociedad
who eventually takes everything
you are worth
and treats it like a commodity
for sale on the common market.

Bato Loco! Wake up.
Anachronism is not your dessert.
Pan dulce y chocolate
sounds better! No?
Levántate, bato loco, levántate
and begin to see the world around you.

"Race" Politics

BY LUIS J. RODRÍGUEZ

My brother and I
—shopping for *la jefita*—
decided to get the "good food"
over on the other side
    of the tracks.

We dared each other.
Laughed a little.
Thought about it.
Said, what's the big deal.
Thought about that.
Decided we were men,
not boys.
Decided we should go wherever
we damn wanted to.

Oh, my brother—now he was bad.
Tough dude. Afraid of nothing.
I was afraid of him.

So there we go,
climbing over
the iron and wood ties,
over discarded sofas
    and bent-up market carts,
over a weed-and-dirt road,
into a place called South Gate
—all white. All-American.

We entered the forbidden
narrow line of hate,
imposed,
transposed,
supposed,
a line of power/powerlessness
full of meaning,
meaning nothing—
those lines that crisscross
the abdomen of this land,
that strangle you
in your days, in your nights.
When you dream.

There we were, two Mexicans,
six and nine—from Watts, no less.
Oh, this was plenty reason
to hate us.

Plenty reason to run up behind us.
Five teenagers on bikes.
Plenty reason to knock
the groceries out from our arms—
    a splattering heap of soup
    cans, bread and candy.

Plenty reason to hold me down
on the hot asphalt; melted gum
    and chips of broken
    beer bottle on my lips and cheek.

Plenty reason to get my brother
by the throat, taking turns
    punching him in the face,
    cutting his lower lip,
    punching, him vomiting.

Punching until swollen and dark blue
he slid from their grasp
like a rotten banana from its peeling.

When they had enough, they threw us back,
dirty and lacerated,
back to Watts, its towers shiny
across the orange-red sky.

My brother then forced me
to promise not to tell anybody
how he cried.
He forced me to swear to God,
to Jesus Christ, to our long-dead
Indian Grandmother—
keepers of our meddling souls.

Política "racial"
Translated from the English by Lori M. Carlson

Mi hermano y yo
—de compras para "la jefita"—
decidimos buscar "la buena comida"
en otra clase de barrio.

Nos desafiamos el uno al otro.
Nos reímos un poco.
Lo pensamos.
Dijimos ¿y por qué no?
Y pensamos aún más.
Decidimos que éramos hombres,
no niños.
Decidimos que debíamos ir
donde se nos antojara.

Mi hermano—sí que era malo.
Un chota. No tenía miedo de nada.
Yo tenía miedo de él.

De modo que ahí vamos
trepando sobre
rieles de madera y hierro,
sobre sofás abandonados
      y changuitos averiados
sobre un camino lleno de malezas,
hacia un lugar llamado South Gate
—todo blanco. All-American.

Cruzamos la estrecha línea
prohibida del odio,
impuesta,
transpuesta,
supuesta,
una línea de poder/sin poder
plena de significado
que nada significa—
esas líneas que cruzan
el estómago de esta tierra,
que te estrangulan
en tus días, en tus noches.
Cuando sueñas.

Allí estábamos, dos mejicanos,
de seis y nueve años—de Watts, nada menos.
Oh, ésta era una razón más que suficiente
para odiarnos.

Suficiente razón para correr tras nosotros
cinco adolescentes en bicicleta.
Suficiente razón para quitarnos
las compras de nuestros brazos—
	un montón chapoteado de latas
	de sopa, pan y dulces.

Suficiente razón para arrojarme
sobre el asfalto caliente; chicle derretido
	y pedazos de botellas de cerveza
	en mis labios y mejillas.

Suficiente razón para agarrar a mi hermano
por la garganta, turnándose para
	golpearlo en la cara
	para cortar su labio inferior,
	puñetazos y él que vomita.

Puñetazos hasta que se hincha y se pone azul
se les escapó de las manos
como una banana podrida de su cáscara.

Cuando se cansaron
nos echaron
sucios y lacerados
de nuevo a Watts, sus torres brillantes
contra el cielo rosa-anaranjado.

Entonces mi hermano me obligó
a prometerle que no contaría a nadie
de cómo él había llorado.
Me obligó a jurar por Dios,
por Jesucristo, por nuestra abuela india muerta
hace tiempo—
guardianes de nuestras almas entrometidas.

Niggerlips
BY MARTÍN ESPADA

Niggerlips was the high school name
for me.
So called by Douglas
the car mechanic, with green tattoos
on each forearm,
and the choir of round pink faces
that grinned deliciously
from the back row of classrooms,
droned over by teachers
checking attendance too slowly.

Douglas would brag
about cruising his car
near sidewalks of black children
to point an unloaded gun,
to scare niggers
like crows off a tree,
he'd say.

My great-grandfather Luis
was un negrito too,
a shoemaker in the coffee hills
of Puerto Rico, 1900.
The family called him a secret
and kept no photograph.
My father remembers
the childhood white powder
that failed to bleach
his stubborn copper skin,

and the family says
he is still a fly in milk.

So Niggerlips has the mouth
of his great-grandfather,
the song he must have sung
as he pounded the leather and nails,
the heat that courses through copper,
the stubbornness of a fly in milk,
and all you have, Douglas,
is that unloaded gun.

Negro Bembón
Translated from the English
by Camilo Pérez-Bustillo with Martín Espada

Negro Bembón es lo que me llamaban
en la secundaria.
Así me decía Douglas,
el mecánico de carros, con sus tatuajes verdes
en cada antebrazo,
y el coro de caras rosadas redondas
que se sonreían con gusto
desde las filas traseras de las aulas,
mientras maestros zumbaban sobre ellas
revisando la asistencia con demasiada lentitud.

Douglas se jactaba
de guiar su auto
cerca de aceras llenas de niños negros
para encañonarlos con una arma descargada,
para asustar negros malditos
como si fueran cuervos espantados
de un árbol,
decía.

Mi bisabuelo Luis
era un negrito también,
un zapatero entre los cafetales
de Puerto Rico, 1900.
La familia lo consideraba un secreto
y no conservaba ninguna foto suya.
Mi padre recuerda
el polvo blanco de la niñez
que no le sirvió para blanquear

su indomable piel cobriza,
y la familia dice
que es aún una mosca en la leche.

Entonces el Negro Bembón tiene la boca
de su bisabuelo,
la canción que él habrá cantado
al martillar el cuero y los clavos,
el calor que fluye por el cobre,
la terquedad de una mosca en la leche,
y lo único que tienes tú, Douglas,
es esa arma descargada.

Excerpts from "Smokey"

*The following two poems are part of a larger work
also called "Smokey."*

La Novia

BY RICARDO MEANS YBARRA

"It was just a birthday party," she told the reporter.
"There were no problems 'til the chotas came.
"He didn't do nothing. He was trying to calm them down."

Lanterns, a string of them across the porch
plugged-in Japanese lanterns
thumbtacks to hold them in place.
When one swung loose
she could feel it drop
that's what made her look
made her turn from his shoulder
where he had attached her
three days out of road camp
three days of love
Poco a poco, they were getting closer
but the swinging lantern
the party had to be right
only three days when she pulled away from him
felt the electric charge off his skin
not wanting him to help
on the porch
the lantern in her hand
thumbtack between fingers
pressed into skin when they came
when she screamed his name
the lantern glow in her hand
only three days of love.

La novia
Translated from the English
by Eugenio Alberto Cano Correa

"Sólo era una fiesta de cumpleaños," le dijo al reportero.
"No hubo ningún problema hasta que vinieron los chotas.
"El no hizo nada. Sólo estaba tratando de calmarlos."

Linternas, una cuerda de ellas atravesando el pórtico
Linternas japonesas enchufadas
tachuelas para mantenerlas en su lugar.
Cuando una se desprendió
ella pudo sentirlo
eso es lo que la hizo mirar
la hizo apartarse de su hombro
donde él la había sostenido
tres días fuera del "road camp"
tres días de amor
Poco a poco estaban intimando
pero la linterna se mecía
la fiesta tenía que ser buena
Bastaron tres días para que ella se apartara de él
sintiera la descarga eléctrica en su piel
no queriendo que él la ayudara
en el pórtico
con la linterna en su mano
tachuela entre los dedos
clavados en su piel cuando llegaron
cuando ella gritó su nombre
el resplendor en su mano
sólo bastaron tres días de amor.

Smokey

BY RICARDO MEANS YBARRA

My name is Arturo Jiménez, a.k.a. Smokey with my homeys
You don't know me, do you?
I was shot in the chest at a birthday party
three days after the Rodney King beating
three days out of road camp
three days back with my girl.
They left me on the sidewalk, called it crowd control
wouldn't let the ambulance through
I don't know but I think I was already dead
'cause all I remember is the Virgen
trying to calm the sheriff
trying to hold back his finger.
Nineteen years old.
Poco a poco, I'm getting closer to you.

Smokey
Translated from the English
by Eugenio Alberto Cano Correa

Me llamo Arturo Jiménez, también conocido por mis
   carnales
como Smokey.
¿No me conoces, verdad?
Me abalaron en el pecho en una fiesta de cumpleaños
tres días después de la golpiza de Rodney King
tres días fuera del *road camp*
tres días después de estar con mi novia.
Me dejaron en la acera, dijeron que era un control policial
no dejaron pasar la ambulancia
No sé pero creo que ya estaba muerto
porque lo único que recuerdo es la Virgen
tratando de calmar al alguacil
tratando de contener sus dedos.
Tenía diecinueve años.
Poco a poco, me acerco a ti.

Time to Party

Nothing but Drums

BY OSCAR HIJUELOS

And now nothing but drums,
a battery of drums, the conga drums jamming out,
in a *descarga*,
and the drummers lifting their heads and
shaking under some kind of spell.
There's rain drums, like pitter-patter pitter-patter
but a hundred times faster, and then
slamming-the-door-drums
and dropping-the-bucket-drums, kicking-the-car-fender
drums. Then circus drums,
then coconuts-falling-out-of-the-trees-and
thumping-against-the-ground-drums, then lion-skin drums,
then the-whacking-of-a-hand-against-a-wall drums,
the beating-of-a-pillow drums, heavy-stones-against-a-wall
   drums,
then the-mountain-rumble drums, then the-little-birds-
   learning
to-fly drums and the big-birds-alighting-on-a-rooftop
and fanning-their-immense-wings drums, then a-boat
down-the-river-with
its-oars-dropping-heavily
into-the-water
drums.

Sólo oye tambores
Translated from the English
by Alejandro García Reyes

Y ahora sólo oye tambores,
una batería de tambores, congas retumbando sonoramente,
en una descarga,
y los percusionistas levantan la cabeza y
se agitan como si tocaran bajo una especie de hechizo.
Hay tambores que suenan como la lluvia, tic-tac, tic-tac
pero cien veces más deprisa, y otros que
suenan como portazos
cubos que caen al suelo, o como puntapiés dados a los
parachoques de un coche. Y también hay tambores de circo,
tambores que suenan como cocos cayendo de los árboles y
estrellandose contra el suelo, tambores de piel de león,
tambores sonando como una fuerte palmada en la pared, o
    como
cuando se golpea una almohada para ahuecarla, o se
lanzan gruesos pedruscos contra una pared;
tambores resonantes como troncos de árboles en la espesura
    del bosque;
como el fulgor de las montañas;
tambores que suenan como pajarillos aprendiendo a volar o
como grandes pajarracos posandose sobre un tejado y
moviendose sus gigantescas alas como si fueran abanicos;
tambores que suenan como una barca arrastrada
río abajo
sin remos que se hunde pesadamente
en el agua.

Mango Juice

BY PAT MORA

Eating mangoes
on a stick
is laughing
as gold juice
slides down
your chin
melting manners,
as mangoes slip
through your lips
sweet but biting

is hitting piñatas
blindfolded and spinning
away from the blues
and grays

is tossing
fragile *cascarones*
on your love's hair,
confetti teasing him
to remove his tie
coat and shoes
his mouth open
and laughing
as you glide
more mango in,
cool rich flesh
of *México*

music teasing
you to strew
streamers on trees
and cactus
teasing the wind
to stream through
your hair blooming
with confetti
and butterflies

your toes warm
in the sand.

Jugo de mango

Translated from the English
by María Rosa Fort

Comer mangos
en un palillo
es reír
mientras un jugo dorado
resbala sobre
tu mentón
derritiendo modales
mientras mangos
se escurren entre tus labios
dulces pero quemantes

es golpear piñatas
con los ojos vendados y girar
lejos de los azules
y los grises

es lanzar
frágiles *cascarones*
al cabello de tu amado,
confetti provocándolo
para quitarle su corbata
abrigo y zapatos
su boca abierta
y riendo
mientras le deslizas
más mango
rica pulpa fresca
de México

música provocándote
a salpicar
de banderolas los árboles
y cactus
provocando al viento
a flamear entre
tus cabellos florecientes
con confetti
y mariposas

los dedos de tus pies tibios
en la arena.

Nothing More
Translated from the Spanish by Lori M. Carlson

We're dancing
our arms forgotten
my tight
embrace
just my fingertips
nothing but this sea of skin
I'm touching
and the flow of our bodies
toward one side
forward
our two move forward
and the half turn
yearning
quiet, rapture.

Nada más

BY ALFREDO CHACÓN

Tú y yo bailando
los brazos olvidados
el abrazo
estrecho
sólo la punta de los dedos
nada más este campo de piel
que estoy tocando
y el caudal de los cuerpos
hacia un lado
hacia adelante
los dos hacia adelante
y la media vuelta
ansiosa
de quietud y rapto.

Brown Girl, Blonde Okie

BY GARY SOTO

Jackie and I cross-legged
In the yard, plucking at
Grass, cupping flies
And shattering them against
Each other's faces—
Smiling that it's summer,
No school, and we can
Sleep out under stars
And the blink of jets
Crossing up our lives.
The flies leave, or die,
And we are in the dark,
Still cross-legged,
Talking not dogs or baseball,
But whom will we love,
What brown girl or blonde
Okie to open up to
And say we are sorry
For our faces, the filth
We shake from our hair,
The teeth without direction.
"We're ugly," says Jackie
On one elbow, and stares
Lost between jets
At what this might mean.
In the dark I touch my
Nose, trace my lips, and pinch
My mouth into a dull flower.
Oh God, we're in trouble.

Chica morena, campesina rubia
Translated from the English
by Luis Alberto Ambroggio

Jackie y yo cruzados de piernas
En el jardín, arrancando
Grama, atrapando moscas
Y aplastándolas contra
Nuestras caras—
Sonriendo porque es verano
Sin escuela y podemos
Dormir afuera bajo las estrellas
Y el parpadeo de los jets
Cruzando nuestras vidas.
Las moscas se van o mueren
Y nosotros estamos en la oscuridad.
Todavía cruzados de piernas.
Hablando no de perros ni de béisbol
Sino de a quién amaremos,
A cuál chica morena o campesina
Rubia nos confiaremos
Y le pediremos perdón
Por nuestras caras, la suciedad
Que sacudimos de nuestro cabello,
Los dientes sin dirección.
''Somos feos,'' dice Jackie
Apoyado en un codo, y contempla
Perdido entre los jets
A lo que esto podría significar.
En la oscuridad yo toco mi
Nariz, bordeo mis labios y aprieto
Mi boca formando una insípida flor.
¡Ay Dios, qué problema!

Why Do Men Wear Earrings on One Ear?

BY TRINIDAD SÁNCHEZ, JR.

Sepa yo!
Maybe por costumbre, maybe porque es la moda
or they have made promesas, maybe for some vieja
for cosmetics or because some women love it
because they were on sale
because they are egocentric cabrones y buscan la atención
because la chica selling them was sooooo mamacita
and they could not refuse
maybe to tell you they are free, innovative, avant-garde
and liberated, maybe because of the full moon
because one earring is cheaper than two
maybe to keep the women guessing
and the men on their toes
maybe they are gay caballeros
maybe as a reminder de algo que no querían olvidar—
like the last time they had sex or to be sexy-looking
maybe they are sexually confused
maybe to let *you* know they are very easily sexually aroused
maybe to separate themselves from los más machos
maybe they are poets, writers
y la literatura is their thing!

Why do men wear earrings on one ear?
Sepa yo! Maybe baby . . .
they are reincarnated pirutos of yesteryear
maybe they lost the other one
maybe they are looking for someone good at cooking

maybe it makes them look like something is cooking
maybe to send signals—the left ear is right
and the right ear is wrong
maybe it depends on which coast you are on.

Why do men wear earrings on one ear?
Who knows . . . maybe it looks much better
than the nose, the toes
maybe to remind others which ear is deaf
maybe to distinguish them from those who don't
and those who won't,
maybe to separate them from the women
maybe because as some women say:
men can only do things half right
maybe to be imitators of the superior sex—halfway
maybe they are undercover policía trying to be *real* cool
maybe they are Republicans trying to be
progressively liberal
maybe they are Democrats disguising their conservatism
or leftists telling you they are in the right party
or revolutionaries looking for a peace—P E A C E!

Maybe they are undecided
maybe to be cute
maybe because life is short.

Why do men wear earrings on one ear?
Sepa yo!

For Ray

BY ANA CASTILLO

i found a stash of records
at the Old Town Street Fair.
Gave up Pérez Prado,
"Rey del Mambo,"
to Ray.

But Cal Tjader's
Soul Sauce
Guacha Guaro
cooler than
a summer's night breeze—
Della Reese in spaghetti strap
dress cha-cha-cha—
is *mine*.

And who am I?
A kid on the güiro
who no one saw jamming
scrawny and scabby kneed
didn't sing Cucurrucucú Paloma
or Cielito Lindo but happy
to mambo
please to teach ya
all of seven then . . .

Now, with timbales
and calloused hands
not from a career of
one-night stands but the grave
yard shift on a drill press,

Ray thrills the children
who slide in party shoes
at Grandpa's house where
the music blares and it's
all right guacha guaro
guacha guaro it's all right.
My daddy's still *cool.*

Para Ray
Translated from the English by María Rosa Fort

Encontré un escondite de discos
en la Old Town Street Fair.
Renuncié a Pérez Prado,
"Rey del Mambo,"
por Ray.

Pero Cal Tjader
su Soul Sauce
Guacha Guaro
más *cool* que
la brisa de una noche de verano—
Della Reese con spaghetti strap
vestido cha-cha-chá—
es *mío*.

¿Y quién soy yo?
Una chica en el güiro
a quien nadie vio improvisando
huesuda y con rodillas peladas
no canté Cucurrucucú Paloma
o Cielito Lindo pero feliz
de bailar mambo
un placer enseñarte
tenía siete años entonces . . .

Ahora, con timbales
y manos callosas
no por una carrera de aventuras
de una noche sino por el turno
de medianoche en un taladro,

Ray deleita a los niños
que se deslizan en zapatos de fiesta
por la casa del abuelo donde
la música retumba and it's
all right guacha guaro
guacha guaro it's all right.
Mi papi todavía es *cool*.

Aquatic Show
Translated from the Spanish by Lori M. Carlson

I make
a complete spectacle
of myself
in the morning shower.
Perhaps more than—
if you forgive me for saying so—
Álvarez Guedes.
I am
a one-man band;
I'm a tenor
baritone
soprano
a chorus of
falsetto voices;
or only a percussion group
African, Antillean
or mixed
according to your pleasure.

I specialize
in good old songs
Argentine
Mexican
naturally Colombian
and a few
Peruvian
Chilean?
I only know one
and Bolivian?
none.

But for the Grand Finale
I reserve
my version
of Joropo's "Carmen Tea"
accompanied by clapping
on my thighs
my butt
my chest
which deeply delight
the *anima mea.*

Espectáculo acuático

BY DANIEL JÁCOME ROCA

Soy
todo un espectáculo
en el baño matutino.
Mejor,
con el perdón del reputado,
que Álvarez Guedes.
Soy
un hombre orquesta;
soy un tenor
un barítono
una soprano
un coro
de voces falsetto;
o tan sólo un conjunto de percusión
africano, antillano
o mixto
al gusto del consumidor.

Me especializo
en cantos antiguos
argentinos
mexicanos,
por supuesto colombianos
y uno que otro
peruano
Chilenos
sólo sé uno
y bolivianos
ninguno.

Pero siempre reservo
para el "Gran Finale"
mi versión
del Joropo "Carmen Tea"
acompañado de palmadas
en los muslos
en las nalgas
y en el pecho
que causan indeleble gozo
en el *anima mea*.

A Promising Future

Why Am I So Brown?

BY TRINIDAD SÁNCHEZ, JR.

for Raquel Guerrero

A question Chicanitas sometimes ask
while others wonder: Why is the sky blue
or the grass so green?

Why am I so Brown?

God made you brown, mi'ja
color bronce—color of your raza
connecting you to your raíces,
your story/historia
as you begin moving towards your future.

God made you brown, mi'ja
color bronce, beautiful/strong,
reminding you of the goodness
de tu mamá, de tus abuelas
y tus antepasados.

God made you brown, mi'ja
to wear as a crown for you are royalty—
a princess, la raza nueva,
the people of the sun.

It is the color of Chicana women—
leaders/madres of Chicano warriors
luchando por la paz y la dignidad
de la justicia de la nación, Aztlán!

God wants you to understand . . . brown
is not a color . . . it is:
a state of being a very human texture
alive and full of song, celebrating—
dancing to the new world
which is for everyone . . .

Finally, mi'ja
God made you brown
because it is one of HER favorite colors!

Solidarity
Translated from the Spanish by Lori M. Carlson

Lark, let's sing!
Waterfall, jump!
Brook, let's run!
Diamond, shine!
Eagle, let's fly!
Dawn, be born!
> Singing!
> Jumping!
> Running!
> Shining!
> Flying!
> We are born!

Solidaridad
BY AMADO NERVO

Alondra, ¡vamos a cantar!
Cascada, ¡vamos a saltar!
Riachuelo, ¡vamos a correr!
Diamante, ¡vamos a brillar!
Águila, ¡vamos a volar!
Aurora, ¡vamos a nacer!
> ¡A cantar!
> ¡A saltar!
> ¡A correr!
> ¡A brillar!
> ¡A volar!
> ¡A nacer!

We Would Like You to Know

BY ANA CASTILLO

We would like you to know
we are not all
docile
nor revolutionaries
but we are all survivors.
We do not all carry
zip guns, hot pistols,
steal cars.
We do know how
to defend ourselves.

We do not all have
slicked-back hair
distasteful apparel
unpolished shoes
although the economy
doesn't allow everyone
a Macy's charge card.

We do not all pick
lettuce, run
assembly lines, clean
restaurant tables, even
if someone has to do it.

We do not all sneak
under barbed wire or
wade the Rio Grande.

These are the facts.

We would like you to know
we are not all brown.
Genetic history has made
some of us blue eyed as any
German immigrant
and as black as a descendant
of an African slave.
We never claimed to be
a homogeneous race.

We are not all victims,
all loyal to one cause,
all perfect; it is a
psychological dilemma
no one has resolved.

We would like to give
a thousand excuses
as to why we all find
ourselves in a predicament
residents of a controversial
power
how we were all caught
with our pants down
and how petroleum was going
to change all that but
you've heard it all before and
with a wink and a snicker
left us babbling amongst
ourselves.

We would like you to know
guilt or apologetic gestures
won't revive the dead
redistribute the land
or natural resources.

We are left
with one final resolution
in our own predestined way,
we are going forward.
There is no going back.

Nos gustaría que sepan
Translated from the English by Johanna Vega

Nos gustaría que sepan
que no todos somos
dóciles
ni revolucionarios
sino que somos todos sobrevivientes.
No todos llevamos
pistolas o revólveres
ni robamos carros.
Sí sabemos cómo
defendernos.

No todos tenemos
el pelo engrasado hacia atrás
ni mal gusto en la ropa
ni zapatos sin brillo
aunque la economía
no permita que todo el mundo tenga
una tarjeta de crédito en Macy's.

No todos recogemos
la lechuga ni trabajamos
en líneas de montaje ni limpiamos
las mesas de los restaurantes, aunque
alguien deba hacerlo.

No todos nos escabullimos
bajo alambres de púas ni
vadeamos el Río Grande.

He aquí los hechos.

Nos gustaría que sepan
que no todos somos morenos.
La historia genética nos ha dado
ojos azules como cualquier otro
inmigrante alemán
y negros como él de un descendiente
de esclavo africano.
Nunca pretendimos
ser una raza homogénea.

No todos somos víctimas
ni todos fieles a una causa,
ni todos perfectos; es un
dilema psicológico que
nadie ha resuelto.

Nos gustaría dar
mil excusas
de por qué todos nos
encontramos en una situación difícil
residentes de un poder
controversial
de cómo fuimos encontrados
con nuestros pantalones en el piso
y de cómo el petróleo iba

a cambiar todo pero
ya han oído eso antes y
con un guiño y una risa sarcástica
nos dejaron con una cháchara
entre nosotros.

Nos gustaría que sepan
que ni la culpa ni las apologías
resucitarán a los muertos
ni van a reapartir las tierras
o los recursos naturales.
Sólo nos queda
una resolución final
a nuestro propio modo predestinado,
seguir adelante.
No se puede retroceder.

Return

*Translated from the Spanish
by Lori M. Carlson*

Yesterdays: do not return
remain
in yesteryear.

Bad dreams: do not come back,
nor good dreams either.

Better that today
shine on tomorrow that
will lead us to the future.

Volver

BY BERTA G. MONTALVO

Que no vuelvan los ayeres
que se quedan así
en ayer.

Que no vuelvan los sueños malos,
ni los buenos tampoco.

Es mejor que el hoy
alumbre un mañana
que no tenga que volver.

Love Poem for My People

BY PEDRO PIETRI

do not let
artificial lamps
make strange shadows
out of you
do not dream
if you want your dreams
to come true
you knew how to sing
before you was
issued a birth certificate
turn off the stereo
this country gave you
it is out of order
your breath
is your promiseland
if you want
to feel very rich
look at your hands
that is where
the definition of magic
is located at

Poema de amor para mi gente
Translated from the English by Alexandra López

no dejes que
lámparas artificiales
hagan de ti
sombras extrañas
no sueñes
si quieres que tus sueños
se hagan realidad
tú sabías cantar
antes de que fuiste
dado un certificado de nacimiento
apaga la radio
que este país te dio
está fuera de servicio
tu aliento
es tu tierra prometida
si quieres
sentirte bien rico
mírate las manos
es ahí donde
la definición de magia
se encuentra

The Calling

BY LUIS J. RODRÍGUEZ

The calling came to me
while I languished
in my room, while I
whittled away my youth
in jail cells
and damp *barrio* fields.

It brought me to life,
out of captivity,
in a street-scarred
and tattooed place
I called body.

Until then I waited silently,
a deafening clamor in my head,
but voiceless to all around;
hidden from America's eyes,
a brown boy without a name.

I would sing into a solitary
        tape recorder,
music never to be heard.
I would write my thoughts
in scrambled English;
I would take photos in my mind—
        plan out new parks,
        bushy green, concrete free,
        new places to play
        and think.

Waiting.
Then it came.
The calling.
It brought me out of my room.
It forced me to escape
night captors
in street prisons.

It called me to war,
to be writer,
to be scientist
and march with the soldiers
        of change.

It called me from the shadows,
out of the wreckage
of my *barrio*—from among those
who did not exist.

I waited all of 16 years
for this time.

Somehow, unexpected,
I was called.

El llamado
Translated from the English
by Patricio Navia

El llamado me llegó
mientras languidecía
en mi cuarto, mientras
me gastaba la juventud
en celdas de cárceles
y húmedos terrenos del barrio.

Me trajo a la vida,
desde el cautiverio,
en una áspera calle
y lugar de tatuajes
que llamaba cuerpo.

Hasta entonces esperé en silencio,
un clamor ensordecedor en mi cabeza,
pero no lo oían los que estaban a mi alrededor;
escondido a los ojos de América,
un niño obscuro, sin nombre.

Cantaba con un radio-cassette solitario
música que nunca sería oída.
Escribía mis ideas
en inglés revuelto;
tomaba fotos en mi mente—
    planeaba nuevos parques;
    con mucho verde, sin cemento.
    Nuevos lugares para jugar
    y pensar.

Esperando.
Luego vino.
El llamado.
Me sacó de mi cuarto.
Me forzó a escapar
de los captores nocturnos
en las prisiones de las calles.

Me llamó a la guerra,
a ser escritor,
a ser científico
y marchar con los soldados
	del cambio.

Me llamó de las sombras,
me sacó de la destrucción
de mi *barrio*—de entre aquéllos
que no existen.

Esperé esos dieciséis años
este momento.

De algún modo, sin que lo esperara,
fui llamado.

Glossary

"English con Salsa"

inglés con chile y cilantro: English with spice
Benito Juárez: President of Mexico from 1857 to 1863 and from 1867 to 1872
Xochicalco: small town in Mexico
dólares and dolores: dollars and pains
Teocaltiche: town in Mexico
English *refrito:* refried English
English *con sal y limón:* English with salt and lemon
requinto from Uruapán: small guitar from the town of Uruapán
mezcal from Juchitán: a strong liquor made from cactus, in this case from the city of Juchitán
amigos del sur: friends from the south
Zapotec: a specific tribe of Mexican Indians
Nahuatl: the Aztecan language
duendes: goblins or ghostly spirits
Santa Tristeza: Saint Sadness
Santa Alegría: Saint Happiness
Santo Todolopuede: Saint All-Powerful
pollo loco: literally, crazy chicken
chapulines: small children
Mixtec: an adjective describing something particular to the Mexican indigenous people known by the same name
la tierra: the earth

"A Puerto Rican Girl's Sentimental Education"

Cantinflas: a famous Mexican comedian
Menudo: a Puerto Rican rock band

"Where You From?"

Soy de aquí/y soy de allá: I'm from here/and I'm from there
del otro lado/y de éste: from the other side/and this side
crecí en L.A./y en Ensenada: I grew up in Los Angeles/and
  Ensenada
naranjas/con chile: oranges/with chile
soy del sur/y del norte: I'm from the south/and the north
crecí zurda/y norteada: I grew up left-handed/and northern
cruzando fron/teras: crossing bor/ders
tartamuda/y mareada: stuttering/and dizzy

"Día de los muertos"

Renacen los huertos/también los muertos: the orchards regenerate/
  and so do the dead
El día de los muertos: the day of the dead
por siete minutos: for seven minutes
podemos platicar: we can talk
con los seres queridos fallecidos: with our loved ones who have
  passed away
abuela: grandmother
camposanto: cemetery
personas non gratas: unacceptable persons or legally unrecognized people
luto: mourning
novenas: the recitation of prayers for nine days, in order to
  request a special favor
puños de tierra: handfuls of dirt

"Domingo Means Scrubbing"

'Amá: short form of the word *mamá*
La llorona: a character in folktales known for "weeping"

"An Unexpected Conversion"

güagüancó: a Cuban dance; an offshoot of the *rumba*
kilos: Cuban slang for pennies

"Bato Loco!"

Bato loco: a wise street person, a dude; the expression has both
   a negative and a positive meaning
con su cabeza/llena de mota: with your brain/filled with marijuana
de sus propios barrios: of your own neighborhoods
sangre: blood
miseria: misery
sus carnales: your brothers, pals
estaban cantando: were singing
las rucas: nice-looking women
el infierno: hell
alma: soul
la avena: oatmeal
una sociedad: a society
pan dulce y chocolate: pastry and chocolate
levántate: wake up

"La Novia"

chotas: cops

"Mango Juice"

cascarones: broken shells

"Brown Girl, Blonde Okie"

Okie: sometimes used to denote a migrant farm worker, especially from Oklahoma

"Why Do Men Wear Earrings on One Ear?"

Sepa yo: How should I know
por costumbre: due to habit
vieja: old woman
cabrones: jerks
buscan la atención: they're looking for attention
mamacita: compliment to a woman, such as real nice or real pretty
caballeros: gentlemen
de algo que no querían olvidar: about something that they didn't want to forget
pirutos: pirates
policía: police

"For Ray"

Guacha Guaro: the title of a popular mambo tune
güiro: a percussion instrument made from a dried gourd
timbales: drums native to Cuba; kettledrums

"Why Am I So Brown?"

mi'ja: truncated form of *mi hija,* "my daughter"
color bronce: bronze color
raza: race
raíces: roots
de tu mamá, de tus abuelas/y tus antepasados: your mother, grandmothers/and ancestors
luchando por la paz y la dignidad/de la justicia de la nación, Aztlán: fighting for the peace and dignity/of justice for the Aztlán nation

Biographical Notes

GINA VALDÉS was born in Los Angeles and raised in Mexico and the United States. She has published a bilingual book of poetry, *Eating Fire*. Her poetry and fiction have appeared in many journals in Mexico, Europe, and the United States. She teaches Chicana/o Literature and Culture at UCLA.

E. J. VEGA, a poet of Cuban heritage, holds an M.F.A. in creative writing from Columbia University. His poems have appeared in numerous anthologies and literary magazines, among them *River Styx*, *Parnassus*, and *Americas Review*. He teaches writing at the Fort Schuyler campus of the State University of New York Maritime College.

SANDRA CISNEROS is among the best-known poets and short story writers of Mexican American heritage writing in the United States today. Perhaps her most popular books are *The House on Mango Street* and *My Wicked, Wicked Ways*. She resides in Texas.

JOHANNA VEGA is an essayist, translator, and poet of Puerto Rican heritage who lives in New York City. Her essay "From the South Bronx to Groton" appeared in the book *Independent Schools, Independent Thinkers*.

LUIS ALBERTO AMBROGGIO is an Argentine poet and businessman who resides in Virginia. Among his published books are *Poemas de amor y vida*, *Hombre del aire*, and *Oda ensimismada*.

SANDRA M. CASTILLO was born in Cuba but now lives in the United States. Her poetry has appeared in *Panhandler* and *Apalachee Quarterly*. She teaches English at Miami Dade Community College.

CRISTINA MORENO graduated from high school in Laredo, Texas, and has attended Laredo Junior College. Her work has appeared in the magazine *Hanging Loose*.

ABELARDO B. DELGADO (Lalo) is an educator, poet, and community organizer. In addition to writing poetry and creating multimedia events such as "Heart of Sky, Heart of Earth," he is the founder of Barrio Publications, which he started to help Chicano writers publish their work. He resides in Colorado.

ALICIA GASPAR DE ALBA grew up in El Paso, Texas, and now lives in California. A Chicana poet, she is the author of the poetry collection *Beggar on the Cordoba Bridge*, which is included in *Three Times a Woman: Chicana Poetry*, and the short story collection *The Mystery of Survival and Other Stories*, and has published short stories and poems in many literary magazines and journals.

JUDITH ORTÍZ COFER, an assistant professor of English and creative writing at the University of Georgia, is the author of *Terms of Survival*, *Silent Dancing: A Partial Remembrance of a Puerto Rican Childhood; The Line of the Sun; and, most recently, The Latin Deli*, a collection of prose and poetry.

EUGENIO ALBERTO CANO CORREA was born in Guatemala to a Salvadoran mother and a Nicaraguan father. In 1981 he moved to New Orleans and now attends Columbia College at Columbia University in New York. He is the editor-in-chief of *Encuentros*, a bilingual literary magazine.

ALFONSO QUIJADA URÍAS is a Salvadoran poet and writer. Among his publications is *Supernatural States*, a collection of poems. His poetry and narratives have appeared in numerous national and foreign anthologies.

CLAUDIA QUIRÓZ, a poet of Bolivian parentage, was born in Washington, D.C., and raised in Virginia. She recently completed her M.F.A. in creative writing at Columbia University. Her poetry has appeared in literary journals, including *River Styx* and *Antaeus*.

PABLO MEDINA, a Cuban-born poet, has lived in the United States since 1960. He is the author of the novel *The Marks of Birth*, and his poetry, prose, and translations have appeared in numerous publications, including *The Antioch Review*, *The American Poetry Review*, and *Linden Lane Magazine*.

CAROLINA HOSPITAL is a Cuban American poet and essayist living in Miami, where she teaches writing and literature at Miami Dade Community College. She is the editor of the anthology *Cuban American Writers: Los atrevidos*. Her fiction, essays, and poetry have appeared in *Americas Review* and *Apalachee Quarterly*, among other magazines.

LUIS J. RODRÍGUEZ is a poet, journalist, and critic whose works have appeared in *The Nation*, the *Los Angeles Times*, and *Poets and Writers*. He is a Carl Sandburg Literary Award winner for nonfiction and a 1992 Lannan Fellow in Poetry. He is also the author of the memoir *Always Running: La Vida Loca, Gang Days in L.A.* He lives in Chicago.

RAMÓN DEL CASTILLO lives in Colorado and works part-time as a columnist for the *Rocky Mountain News*. He has received the Raíces Mestizas Award and was named Newsed Poet Laureate of Denver in 1993.

MARTÍN ESPADA has been awarded both the PEN/Revson Fellowship and the Paterson Poetry Prize for his third book, *Rebellion Is the Circle of a Lover's Hands*. He has worked as a housing lawyer and is now an assistant professor of English at the University of Massachusetts at Amherst.

RICARDO MEANS YBARRA's poetry and fiction have appeared widely in magazines, including *Blue Mesa Review*, *Café Solo*, and *The Kenyon Review*. His first novel, *The Pink Rosary*, was published by Latin American Literary Review Press. He is a fifth-generation Californian.

OSCAR HIJUELOS, born of Cuban parentage, won the 1990 Pulitzer Prize in fiction for the novel *The Mambo Kings Play Songs of Love*, the first American novelist of Hispanic origin to have held this honor. He is the author of two other novels, *Our House in the Last World* and *The Fourteen Sisters of Emilio Montez O'Brien*.

PAT MORA is a poet of Mexican heritage. She has published a number of poetry volumes, including *Borders* and *Chants*, for which she won the Southwest Book Award. She lives in Texas.

ALFREDO CHACÓN, a Venezuelan poet, has published *Palabras asaltantes* and *Decir como es deseado*, among other books.

GARY SOTO was born and raised in Fresno, California. He is the author of many books of poetry and prose, including *The Elements of San Joaquín, Living Up the Street, Baseball in April*, and *Local News*. He has produced several films for Spanish-speaking children, and is the editor of *Pieces of the Heart: New Chicano Fiction*.

TRINIDAD SÁNCHEZ, JR., is a nationally known Chicano poet and author who lectures extensively at schools, universities, and literary and cultural centers. He resides in San Antonio. He is the author of the poetry collection *Why Am I So Brown?* and the chapbooks *Authentic Chicano Food Is Hot* and *Father and Son*.

ANA CASTILLO, a well-known Chicana novelist and poet, has published many books of poetry, among them *My Father Was a Toltec* and *Women Are Not Roses*, and the novel *So Far from God*. She resides in Florida.

DANIEL JÁCOME ROCA is a Colombian poet and physician who resides in Miami. His work has appeared in *Linden Lane Magazine* and other publications.

AMADO NERVO, a prolific Mexican writer of poetry and prose, was one of the best-known modernist poets of the Spanish-speaking world. He died in 1919.

122

BERTA G. MONTALVO, who was born in La Habana, Cuba, lives in Miami. Among her published works are *Para mi gaveta*, *Miniaturas*, and *Gotas de rocío*.

PEDRO PIETRI, a major Puerto Rican poet living in New York City, is perhaps best known for his collection *Puerto Rican Obituary*.